First Steps To Understanding

Balagah

Hashim Muhammad

Al-Qalam Publications

First Steps To Understanding Balagah
First Edition April, 2016

ISBN: 978-0-9576534-7-4

Compiler   Hashim Muhammad

Contact: Al-Qalam
                    28 Melbourne Road,
                    Leicester, LE2 0DR,
                    United Kingdom
Email: info@alqalaminstitute.org
Website: http://alqalaminstitute.org
Mobile/WhatsApp   +44 7507859443

If you see any mistakes in this book, have any comments or suggestions, please feel free to contact us. Jazakallah.

Printed by Mega Printing in Turkey

Contents

4

Balagah is one of the important subjects needed to fully appreciate the Quran. This is why it is taught in most of the madaris.

When I first started teaching this subject in madrasah over 10 years ago, دروس البلاغة was used as the text. However, most of the examples used in this book are poems. Unfortunately, most students were not able to properly understand them; and those students who did understand them were not captured in seeing the Balagah in the poetry. To them it seemed as Balagah was a separate subject with no link to Quran and Hadith. To fill this void, I, with the Help of Allah ﷻ, compiled a small book in Arabic which I named البلاغة القرآنية. This was basically the text of دروس البلاغة in which all the examples were replaced with examples from the Quran.

However, after teaching this book to beginners for a few years, I found that even though the students would enjoy the science, at times it was bit too complex to grasp. I felt there was still a need for an easier simpler book which could serve as a very basic introduction to this subject. Hence, I compiled this booklet. It does not go into much detail as its sole purpose is to introduce the subject and give the reader a brief overview of the main topics discussed. For a proper understanding of Balagah, another book needs to be taught after this book.

In this booklet we are going to study the very basics of Balagah.

الْبَلَاغَة means to use فصيح words in a sentence with correct grammar in an appropriate and suitable manner.

فصيح means correct and appropriate words. i.e. it conforms the rules of Sarf and Nahw.

Imagine you were giving a lecture. This requires you to elaborate and give detail. If you were calling for an ambulance, you would need to be brief and precise. In both scenarios you would need to use correct language. If you use correct language in the correct manner this is called بَلاغة. Many of the concepts of Balagah are not exclusive to Arabic and are found in other languages. Balagah is broken down into three main sections:

1) عِلْمُ الْمَعَانِي
2) عِلْمُ الْبَيَانِ
3) عِلْمُ الْبَدِيْعِ

Section One

علْمُ الْمَعَانِي

The first section of Balagah is called عِلْمُ الْمَعَانِيْ. This is regarding those rules of Nahw which influence the meaning of sentence, not the إعراب. For example, you have learnt two words that translate as when: مَتٰى and أَيَّانَ; in Nahw you would study about them being مبني or معرب etc. In علم المعاني, we will learn things regarding their different meanings and when each should be used.

In this section we will discuss the following topics:

1) Parts of a Sentence.
2) Types of Sentences.
3) Sentence Order.
4) Details of معرفة and نكرة.
5) Creating Restrictions.
6) A Few Details About حرف العطف.
7) Length of Speech.
8) A Few Miscellaneous Rules.

Discussion 1
Parts of A Sentence

In any language a sentence must have a subject. In Arabic this is called مُسْنَدٌ إِلَيْهِ. This includes both the مبتدأ and فاعل.

The information you give regarding the subject is called مُسْنَدٌ. This can either be خبر or فعل.

These are the two main parts of a sentence. Everything else is extra, قَيْد. Extra here means the grammar of the sentence would be complete without it even though the meaning may not be.

Look at the following example:

﴿لَا تَقْرَبُوا الصَّلَاةَ وَأَنْتُمْ سُكَارَى﴾[نساء: ٤٣]

Do not go near Salah when you are intoxicate.

In this sentence, the sentence وأنتم سكارى is حال, which is a قَيْد.

The grammar of the sentence is complete without it, but obviously the meaning would completely change. In fact, the قُيُود (plural of قيد) are the focal point of the sentences. Without these the sentence would not give the desired meaning.

The قُيُود are as follows:

1) مفعول به

﴿وَإِذِ ابْتَلَى إِبْرَاهِيمَ رَبُّهُ﴾[البقرة: ١٢٤]

When his Lord put Ibrahim to a test...

2) مفعول مطلق

﴿فَلَا تَمِيلُوا كُلَّ الْمَيْلِ﴾[النساء: ١٢٩]

So, do not lean totally [towards one wife]...

3) مفعول له

﴿وَلَا تَقْتُلُوا أَوْلَادَكُمْ خَشْيَةَ إِمْلَاقٍ﴾[الإسراء: ٣١]

Do not kill your children for fear of poverty.

4) مفعول فيه

﴿قَالُوا لَبِثْنَا يَوْمًا أَوْ بَعْضَ يَوْمٍ﴾[الكهف: ١٩]

They said, "We have stayed a day, or part of a day."

5) مفعول مع

قَالَ كُنْتُ أَغْتَسِلُ أَنَا وَرَسُولَ اللَّهِ صَلَّى اللَّهُ عَلَيْهِ مِنْ إِنَاءٍ وَاحِدٍ [البخاري]

The Prophet ﷺ and I used to take a bath from one container [of water].

6) حال

﴿لَا تَقْرَبُوا الصَّلَاةَ وَأَنْتُمْ سُكَارَى﴾ [النساء:٤٣]

Do not go near Salah *when you are intoxicated.*

7) تمييز

﴿فَلَنْ يُقْبَلَ مِنْ أَحَدِهِمْ مِلْءُ الْأَرْضِ ذَهَبًا﴾ [آل عمران:٩١]

Even an Earth-*full of gold* shall never be accepted from any of them.

8) مستثنى

﴿الْأَخِلَّاءُ يَوْمَئِذٍ بَعْضُهُمْ لِبَعْضٍ عَدُوٌّ إِلَّا الْمُتَّقِينَ﴾ [الزخرف:٦٧]

Friends, on that day, will become enemies to one another, *except the God-fearing.*

9) النواسخ

﴿وَأَصْبَحَ فُؤَادُ أُمِّ مُوسَى فَارِغًا﴾ [القصص:١٠]

And the heart of the mother of Musa *became restless.*

10) الشرط

﴿وَإِنْ كُنْتُمْ فِي رَيْبٍ مِمَّا نَزَّلْنَا عَلَى عَبْدِنَا فَأْتُوا بِسُورَةٍ مِنْ مِثْلِهِ﴾ [البقرة:٢٣]

If you are in doubt about what We have revealed to Our servant then bring a Surah similar to this.

11) النفي

﴿أَلَيْسَ اللَّهُ بِأَحْكَمِ الْحَاكِمِينَ﴾ [التين:٨]

Is Allah *not the* Greatest Ruler of all the rulers?

They are two types of sentences:

1) جُمْلَةٌ خَبَرِيَّةٌ: This is a sentence in which some kind of information is being stated.

﴿الْحَمْدُ لِلَّهِ رَبِّ الْعَالَمِينَ﴾ [الفاتحة:١]

Praise belongs to Allah.

2) جُمْلَةٌ إِنْشَائِيَّةٌ: This is a sentence where information is not stated, rather something like a command is issued.

﴿اهْدِنَا الصِّرَاطَ الْمُسْتَقِيمَ﴾ [الفاتحة:٥]

Take us on the straight path.

الجملة الخبرية

There are two types of جملة خبرية:

1) جُمْلَةٌ إِسْمِيَّةٌ: This is a sentence which does not have a verb. It is important to note this differs from the Nahw definition of جملة إسمية. In Balagah terminology, if a sentence has a فعل in it, it will be considered to be the same as a جملة فعلية, unlike Nahw.

The purpose of جملة إسمية is to show that a link exists between the مبتدأ and خبر. This is called ثُبُوْت.

الدَّرْسُ سَهْلٌ

The lesson is easy.

Sometimes the context of a sentence will show that the link is long term. This is called دَوَام.

﴿اللهُ رَبُّ الْعَالَمِينَ﴾ [الأعراف:٥٤]

Allah is the lord of the worlds.

11

If كان comes with a جملة إسمية it shows that the link existed in the past.

﴿إِنَّ إِبْرَاهِيمَ كَانَ أُمَّةً﴾ [النحل: ١٢٠]

Surely, Ibrahim was an Ummah.

2) جُمْلَةٌ فِعْلِيَّةٌ: This is a sentence which has a verb in it. This can be split into two types:

    a. A sentence with فعل ماض. The purpose of this type of sentence is to show that an action took place. This is called حُدُوث.

﴿وَقَتَلَ دَاؤُودُ جَالُوتَ﴾ [البقرة: ٢٥١]

And Dawud (David) killed Golliath.

    b. A sentence with فعل مضارع. The purpose of this type of sentence is to show one of two things:
    i) an action takes place continuously

﴿وَاللَّهُ يَرْزُقُ مَنْ يَشَاءُ بِغَيْرِ حِسَابٍ﴾ [البقرة: ٢١٢]

Allah gives whom He wills without counting.

This is called تَجَدُّد.

ii) an action will take place in the future.

﴿ثُمَّ يَأْتِي مِنْ بَعْدِ ذَلِكَ سَبْعٌ شِدَادٌ﴾ [يوسف: ٤٨]

Then after that will come seven hard years.

This is also called حُدُوث.

Notes:

1. حُدُوث comes for both past and future.

2. If كان comes with a فعل مضارع it will give the meaning of تجدد in the past i.e. past habitual.

﴿كَانَا يَأْكُلَانِ الطَّعَامَ﴾[المائدة : ٧٥]

Both of them used to eat food.

Sentence Types		
جملة إسمية	جملة فعلية ماضوية	جملة فعلية مضارعية
Original Meaning ثبوت	حدوث	تجدد حدوث
Possible Meaning With Context دوام		
With كان ثبوت في الماضي		تجدد في الماضي

The following example shows how the different types of sentences affect the meaning.

﴿وَإِذَا لَقُوا الَّذِينَ آمَنُوا قَالُوا آمَنَّا وَإِذَا خَلَوْا إِلَى شَيَاطِينِهِمْ قَالُوا إِنَّا مَعَكُمْ﴾[البقرة :١٤]

When they [the hypocrites] meet those who believe, they say, "We have entered Faith;" but when they are alone with their satans, they say, "Indeed, we are with you."

In this verse we have two sentences: one is جملة إسمية and one is جملة فعلية. The reason a different style is used for both is that when the hypocrites proclaim their faith it is hypocritical, there is no ثبوت to it; hence the word آمنا is used to show حدوث i.e. they just showed their faith. However, when they express their association with the satans, they use الجملة الإسمية to show the strength of their relationship i.e. دوام.

13

We are going to discuss 5 types of جُمْلَةٌ إِنْشَائِيَّةٌ:

1) أَمْرٌ

2) نَهْيٌ

3) اِسْتِفْهَامٌ

4) تَمَنٍّ

5) نِدَاءٌ

أمر

This is when that a person who assumes himself to be in authority issues an order to someone lower in rank to him.

There are four ways of giving an order:

1) صِيغَةُ الأَمْرِ

﴿خُذِ الْكِتَابَ بِقُوَّةٍ﴾[مريم:١٢]

Hold fast to the Scripture.

2) صِيغَةُ الأَمْرِ لِلْغَائِب

﴿لِيُنْفِقْ ذُو سَعَةٍ مِنْ سَعَتِهِ﴾[الطلاق:٧]

A man of vast means should spend according to his vast means.

3) الْمَصْدَرُ

«صَبْرًا يَا آلَ يَاسِرٍ» [مستدرك الحاكم]

Be patient, O family of Yasir!

4) إِسْمُ الْفِعْلِ

﴿هَاؤُمُ اقْرَءُوا كِتَابِيَهْ﴾[الحاقة:١٩]

Come here! Read my book.

14

هِيَ

There are two ways of giving a negative order:

1) صِيْغَةُ النَّهْي

﴿لَا تُشْرِكْ بِي شَيْئًا﴾[الحج:٢٦]

Do not associate anything with Me as My partner.

2) صِيْغَةُ النَّهْي لِلْغَائِبِ

﴿وَلَا يَأْتَلِ أُولُو الْفَضْلِ مِنْكُمْ وَالسَّعَةِ أَنْ يُؤْتُوا أُولِي الْقُرْبَى وَالْمَسَاكِينَ﴾[النور:٢٢]

The men of grace and wealth among you should not swear against giving [their charitable gifts] to the kinsmen and the poor...

اِسْتِفْهَامٌ

This means to ask a question. You should have studied the details of these in Nahw. Below is a brief recap of the particles of استفهام.

	Meaning	Example
أ	Is/Are	﴿أَأَنْتُمْ أَعْلَمُ أَمِ اللَّهُ﴾[البقرة:١٤٠] *Do you know better or does Allah?*
هَلْ	Is/Are	﴿هَلْ عِنْدَكُمْ مِنْ عِلْمٍ﴾[الأنعام:١٤٨] *Do you have any sure knowledge ...?*
مَا	What	﴿وَمَا تِلْكَ بِيَمِينِكَ يَا مُوسَى﴾[طه:١٧] *And what is that in your right hand, O Musa?*

15

	Meaning	Example
مَنْ	Who	﴿مَنْ أَشَدُّ مِنَّا قُوَّةً﴾[فصلت:١٥] *Who is* **stronger than us in power?**
مَتٰى	When	﴿مَتٰى هَذَا الْوَعْدُ﴾[يونس:٤٨] *When **will this promise ...?***
أَيَّانَ	When	﴿أَيَّانَ يَوْمُ الدِّينِ﴾[الذاريات:١٢] When **shall be the Day of Recompense?**
كَيْفَ	How	﴿كَيْفَ تُحْيِ الْمَوْتَى﴾[البقرة:٢٦٠] How **do You give life to the dead?**
أَيْنَ	Where	﴿أَيْنَ شُرَكَاؤُكُمُ﴾[الأنعام:٢٢] Where **are those you claimed to be partners?**
أَنّٰى	How	﴿أَنّٰى يَكُونُ لَهُ الْمُلْكُ عَلَيْنَا﴾[البَقَرَة:٢٤٧] How **could he have kingship over us?**
	From where	﴿يَا مَرْيَمُ أَنّٰى لَكِ هَذَا﴾[آل عمران:٣٧] Maryam, *from where did* **you have this?**
كَمْ	How many	﴿كَمْ لَبِثْتَ﴾[البقرة:٢٥٩] *How long **did you remain?***
أَيُّ	Which	﴿أَيُّ الْفَرِيقَيْنِ خَيْرٌ مَقَامًا﴾[مريم:٧٣] Which of **the two groups is superior in its place ...?**

This means to desire something which is not possible.

﴿يَا لَيْتَ قَوْمِي يَعْلَمُونَ﴾[يٰس:٢٣]

Would that **my people knew.**

16

The main particle of تمنّ is لیت. This is often preceded by یا which is not translated.

The following particles are also used to express the meaning of تمنّ:

1) هل

﴿فَهَلْ لَنَا مِنْ شُفَعَاءَ فَيَشْفَعُوا لَنَا﴾[الأعراف:٥٣]

So, are there any intercessors for us who could intercede in our favour?

2) لو

﴿لَوْلَا أَخَّرْتَنَا إِلَى أَجَلٍ قَرِيبٍ﴾[النساء:٧٧]

Would you have not spared us for a little more time?

Under the discussion of تمنّ comes the discussion of تَرَجّ i.e. to desire something which is possible.

The following two particles are used to express ترج:

1) عَسٰى

﴿عَسَى اللَّهُ أَنْ يَأْتِيَنِي بِهِمْ جَمِيعًا﴾[يوسف:٨٣]

Hopefully, Allah may bring them all together

2) لَعَلَّ

﴿لَعَلَّ اللَّهَ يُحْدِثُ بَعْدَ ذَلِكَ أَمْرًا﴾[الطلاق:١]

It may be that Allah brings about a new situation thereafter.

نِدَاءٌ

This means to call someone. There are two basic types of نداء:

1) أ or أيْ to call someone who is close .

17

2) يَا to call someone who is far.

﴿يَا آدَمُ﴾ [البقرة:٣٣]

O Adam!

Using خبرية or إنشائية Against its Normal Rules

All of the above mentioned rules and points were things you would have studied in Nahw.

However, many of the above rules are broken to give additional meanings to words and sentences. This is where the intricacies of Balagah start.

As a rule of thumb, remember that when anything is different to the norm, it implies a more dynamic meaning.

Using خبرية Instead of إنشائية and Vice Versa

Sometimes a خبرية is used instead of إنشائية. For example, a مضارع can be used instead of a نهي.

﴿وَإِذْ أَخَذْنَا مِيثَاقَكُمْ لَا تَسْفِكُونَ دِمَاءَكُمْ وَلَا تُخْرِجُونَ أَنْفُسَكُمْ مِنْ دِيَارِكُمْ﴾ [البقرة:٨٤]

When We took a pledge from you: "You shall not shed the blood of one another, and you shall not drive one another out of your homes."

In أمر someone is instructed to do something, and s/he then has a choice to carry it out or not. In مضارع a fact is stated. So by expressing a command in مضارع form, it creates more emphasis by implying that the command is so emphatic that it is a matter of fact and it will be definitely carried out.

18

A جملة إسمية can also be used instead of a نهي.

﴿فَلَا رَفَثَ وَلَا فُسُوقَ وَلَا جِدَالَ فِي الْحَجِّ﴾ [البقرة:١٩٧]

There should be no obscenity, no sin, and no quarrel in Hajj.

The translator has added in the word should to imply that the خبرية is in the meaning of إنشائية i.e. a نهي; however, the real translation is "there is / will be no obscenity, no sin, no quarrel in the Hajj."

On the contrary, an إنشائية maybe used in place of خبرية. This shows the importance of the matter.

﴿أَمَرَ رَبِّي بِالْقِسْطِ وَأَقِيمُوا وُجُوهَكُمْ عِنْدَ كُلِّ مَسْجِدٍ﴾ [الأعراف:٢٩]

My Lord has commanded justice and that you should face Him only [during prayers] in every place of worship.

In this verse there are two commands: to be just and to turn towards Allah ﷻ at the time of prayer. However, the second command is expressed via an إنشائية in a style different to the first. The text should have read like this:

أَمَرَ رَبِّي بِالْقِسْطِ وَأَن تُقِيْمُوا وُجُوهَكُمْ الخ

By changing to إنشائية an emphasis is placed on the second.

Using الماضي Instead of المضارع and Vice Versa

The ماضي shows past tense. This means that the action has already occurred. To show certainty in regards to the occurrence of a future incident الماضي can be used instead of المضارع.

﴿أَتَى أَمْرُ اللَّهِ﴾ [النحل:١]

In this verse, the past tense verb أتى has been used in place of مضارع to show that this will definitely occur. However, it is translated in the future.

The Event ordained by Allah will surely come to pass.

This style is also used in supplications:

جَزَاكَ اللهُ

The literal translation of this is "Allah has rewarded you."

But because الماضي is really in the meaning of future, it is translated with a future tense meaning.

May Allah reward you.

Other Usages of الأمر *and* النهي

When الأمر is used in its original meaning it implies that someone in authority is giving someone inferior a command which is compelling. النهي is the opposite of الأمر.

However, these two have many other meanings apart from this original meaning. Some are:

1) الِيْتِمَاس: Request i.e. the person issuing the الأمر is not in authority and the one being addressed is not inferior.

﴿قَالَ ابْنَ أُمَّ إِنَّ الْقَوْمَ اسْتَضْعَفُونِي وَكَادُوا يَقْتُلُونَنِي فَلَا تُشْمِتْ بِيَ الْأَعْدَاءَ وَلَا تَجْعَلْنِي مَعَ الْقَوْمِ الظَّالِمِينَ﴾

[الأعراف: ١٥٠]

He [Harun] said [to Musa], "My mother's son, the people took me as weak and were about to kill me. So do not let the enemies laugh at me, and do not count me with the wrong-doers."

Haroon ﷺ was not superior to Musa ﷺ, hence his أمر is interpreted as an التماس.

2) إِرْشَادٌ: Advice

﴿يَا أَيُّهَا الَّذِينَ آمَنُوا إِذَا تَدَايَنتُم بِدَيْنٍ إِلَى أَجَلٍ مُّسَمًّى فَاكْتُبُوهُ﴾[البقرة:٢٨٢]

O you who believe, when you transact a debt payable at a specified time, put it in writing.

This الأمر is not compelling, it is only a recommendation.

3) دُعَاء: Prayer

﴿رَبَّنَا تَقَبَّلْ مِنَّا﴾[البقرة:١٢٧]

"Our Lord, accept *[this service] from us!*

4) تَمَنّ: Wish

﴿يَا مَالِكُ لِيَقْضِ عَلَيْنَا رَبُّكَ﴾[الزخرف:٧٧]

"O Malik [warden of the Hell], let your Lord make an end of us."

Here, Allah ﷻ is telling us how the people of hell will beg for death so they may be saved from the punishment. Obviously, they have no authority over the warden of Hell; hence their أمر is a mere whim and fancy.

5) تَسْوِيَة: To show that two things are equal.

﴿فَاصْبِرُوا أَوْ لَا تَصْبِرُوا سَوَاءٌ عَلَيْكُمْ﴾[الطور:٦٢]

Now, whether you endure [it] patiently or impatiently, it is all the same for you.

6) إِبَاحَة: Permission

﴿يَا أَيُّهَا النَّاسُ كُلُوا مِمَّا فِي الْأَرْضِ حَلَالًا طَيِّبًا﴾[البقرة:١٦٨]

O people, eat permissible good things out of what lies in the earth.

Apart from these there are many other usages of الأمر and النهي.

Other Usages of استفهام

The original purpose of استفهام is to ask regarding something in hope of receiving an answer. However, just like in English an استفهام can be **rhetorical** i.e. it is intended for something other than a question. In Arabic, there are different names for the different rhetorical uses of استفهام. Some of these are:

1) أمر: to issue a command

﴿فَهَلْ أَنْتُمْ شَاكِرُونَ﴾ [الأنبياء:٨٠]

So are you grateful?

The purpose of this question is not to receive an answer, rather it is to say "Be grateful".

2) نهي: to issue a prohibition

﴿أَتَخْشَوْنَهُمْ﴾ [التوبة:١٣]

Do you fear them?

i.e don't fear them.

3) تَعَجُّب: to express amazement

﴿وَقَالُوا مَالِ هَذَا الرَّسُولِ يَأْكُلُ الطَّعَامَ وَيَمْشِي فِي الْأَسْوَاقِ﴾ [الفرقان:٧]

What sort of messenger is this who eats food and walks in the markets?

4) تَشْوِيق: to create an interest

﴿هَلْ أَدُلُّكُمْ عَلَى تِجَارَةٍ تُنْجِيكُمْ مِنْ عَذَابٍ أَلِيمٍ﴾ [الصف:١٠]

Shall I tell you about a trade that saves you from a painful punishment?

5) التَّعْظِيم: to show greatness

﴿مَنْ ذَا الَّذِي يَشْفَعُ عِنْدَهُ إِلَّا بِإِذْنِهِ﴾ [البقرة:٢٥٥]

Who can intercede with Him without His permission?

Other Usages of تمن

Normally لَيْت is used for impossible things and لعل for possible things. However, this can be changed around.

﴿وَقَالَ فِرْعَوْنُ يَا هَامَانُ ابْنِ لِي صَرْحًا لَعَلِّي أَبْلُغُ الْأَسْبَابَ أَسْبَابَ السَّمَاوَاتِ فَأَطَّلِعَ إِلَى إِلَهِ مُوسَى﴾ [غافر:٣٦]

And Fir'aun (Pharaoh) said, "O Haman, make a tower for me, perhaps I could reach the ways - The ways to the heavens, and peek towards the God of Musa.

Even though this is something impossible, Fir'aun used the word لعل to give the impression to those around him that is was possible.

Using نداء Contrary to its Normal Rules

Normally a person who is close is addressed via the particle أ. A person who is far is addressed via the particle يا. However, this can be switched around i.e. someone who is close can be addresses via يا and someone far can be addressed via أ. The reason for this would be to show emotional distance.

23

For example, when Musa ﷺ held the beard of his brother Harun ﷺ and reprimanded him for letting the Children of Israel worship the cow, Harun ﷺ replied by saying:

﴿يَبْنَؤُمَّ لَا تَأْخُذْ بِلِحْيَتِي وَلَا بِرَأْسِي﴾ [طه:٩٤]

O son of my mother, do not hold me by my beard, nor by my head.

So even though they were physically close, Harun ﷺ used the word يا to show the distance he felt from his brother.

The منادى itself is usually a name or a word like يا رجلُ. However, if a name is not used, then it is usually for some implicit meaning.

1) إغْرَاءٌ: to urge someone

   After Maryam ﷺ gave birth to Isa ﷺ without a father, she brought him to the people. Their obvious reaction was of amazement and they assumed he was an illegitimate child. They said to her:

   ﴿يَا أُخْتَ هَارُونَ مَا كَانَ أَبُوكِ امْرَأَ سَوْءٍ وَمَا كَانَتْ أُمُّكِ بَغِيًّا﴾ [مريم:٢٨]

   O sister of Harun, neither your father was a man of evil nor was your mother unchaste."

   They addressed her as sister of Harun, to reprimand her that being from such a noble family it was not befitting of her to carry out such an evil (according to their assumption).

2) تَلَطُّف ,مِزَاح: to jest, banter or play around.

24

Once Ali 🕊 had an argument with Fatima 🕊. He stormed out the house and slept in the masjid. When the Prophet 🕊 found out, he came looking for him. Because the masjid was just sand and soil, there was soil on Ali 🕊. The prophet addressed him saying:

يَا أَبَا تُرَابٍ [البخاري]

O Abu Turab (one covered in dust)

3) اَلْإِسْتِهْزَاء: to mock

﴿ وَقَالُوا يَا أَيُّهَا الَّذِي نُزِّلَ عَلَيْهِ الذِّكْرُ إِنَّكَ لَمَجْنُونٌ ﴾ [الحجر:٦]

They say, "O you to whom the Dhikr [the Qur'an] has been revealed, you are surely insane.

The people of Makkah did not believe that revelation came to the Prophet 🕊. Hence this statement of theirs was sarcastic.

Order within A Sentence

In a جملة إسمية the normal order is

مبتدأ – خبر

However, if both the مبتدأ and خبر are معرفة either can be brought first.

﴿اللهُ رَبُّنَا وَرَبُّكُمْ﴾ [الشورى:١٥]

Allah is our Lord and your Lord

In this verse, because both the مبتدأ and خبر are معرفة, from a Nahw perspective it is possible to bring either as مبتدأ. However, the point that is being emphasised will be brought first.

Sometimes the خبر can be brought before the مبتدأ to give emphasis.

﴿لَكُمْ دِينُكُمْ وَلِيَ دِينِ﴾ [الكافرون:٦]

For you is your faith, and for me, my faith.

Bringing something earlier is called تَقْدِيم.

The normal sentence order in a جملة فعلية is

فعل — فاعل — مفعول– متعلق

However, the sentence order can be changed for different reasons:

1) To create emphasis

﴿إِيَّاكَ نَعْبُدُ﴾ [الفاتحة:٥]

*You alone **do we worship***

In this verse, the مفعول is brought first to create an emphasis. This is why *alone* is brought in the translation.

The فاعل can also be brought before the فعل as a مبتدأ to create emphasis.

﴿وَهُمْ يَعْلَمُونَ﴾[البقرة : 75]

whilst they know

2) To keep the rhythm of a sentence.

﴿خُذُوهُ فَغُلُّوهُ ۞ ثُمَّ الْجَحِيمَ صَلُّوهُ ۞ ثُمَّ فِي سِلْسِلَةٍ ذَرْعُهَا سَبْعُونَ ذِرَاعًا فَاسْلُكُوهُ ۞﴾

Seize him, then put a collar around his neck, And then, let him burn in the blazing fire. Thereafter, fasten him with a chain the measure of which is seventy hands.

In the last verse, the متعلق has been brought before the verb to keep the pattern of verses ending in ه.

Order within Parts of A Sentence

If any part of a sentence is made up of two or more words joined via a حرف عطف, one part can be brought before the other for certain reasons.

1) To keep the real order intact.

﴿لَا تَأْخُذُهُ سِنَةٌ وَلَا نَوْمٌ﴾ [البقرة:٢٥٥]

Neither dozing overtakes Him nor sleep.

Dozing comes before sleep, this is why سنة has been brought first.

2) To show hierarchy.

27

﴿يَرْفَعُ إِبْرَاهِيمُ الْقَوَاعِدَ مِنَ الْبَيْتِ وَإِسْمَاعِيلُ﴾ [البقرة:١٢٧]

When Ibrahim was raising up the foundations
of the House, along with Isma'il.

In this verse Ismail ﷺ is brought after Ibrahim ﷺ and even after the مفعول to show that Ibrahim ﷺ was the main builder, and Ismail was helping him.

3) To bring good news first

﴿قَالَ اللهُ يَا عِيسَى إِنِّي مُتَوَفِّيكَ وَرَافِعُكَ﴾ [آل عمران:٥٥]

O 'Isa! I am to take you in full and to raise you
towards Myself

Allah said this to Isa ﷺ when he was surrounded by his enemies who wanted to kill him. The sentence "I am going to take you in full" i.e. give you death first gives assurance that he would not be murdered.

Order within Sentences

Sometimes one sentence maybe brought before another for a particular reason.

﴿عَفَا اللهُ عَنْكَ لِمَ أَذِنْتَ لَهُمْ﴾ [التوبة:٤٣]

O Prophet, Allah has forgiven you; why did you
permit them (to stay in Madinah)

The sentence mentioning the Prophet's ﷺ pardon is mentioned even before mentioning the error. This was done to avoid him worrying about Allah's displeasure.

Discussion 4
Details About نكرة and معرفة

In this discussion we will touch on a few rules regarding the six types of معرفة and some rules about نكرة.

الضمير

A pronoun is used instead of a noun when it has been mentioned previously.

One important note regarding the حاضر pronoun is that it can be used to make a general reference to any person.

«ذِكْرُكَ أَخَاكَ بِمَا يَكْرَهُ» [مسلم]

[Backbiting] is your talking about your brother in a manner which he does not like.

In this hadith, the pronoun you does not refer to a single addressee, rather it applies to any person who hears or reads it.

العَلَم

Names are used when it is the easiest way of talking about someone.

﴿ مُحَمَّدٌ رَسُولُ اللَّهِ﴾[الفتح:٢٩]

Muhammad is the messenger of Allah

However, names can be used to give additional implications if that name carries such a meaning. For example, the name Abu Lahab literally means father of the flame. He was called this because he was very fair skinned with redness in his skin colour. His name is mentioned in the Quran where it fits the punishment he will receive.

﴿ تَبَّتْ يَدَا أَبِي لَهَبٍ وَتَبَّ ... سَيَصْلَى نَارًا ذَاتَ لَهَبٍ﴾[المسد:١-٣]

Perish the two hands of Abu Lahab (the father of the flame), and perish he! … He will soon enter a Fire, full of flames.

اسم الإشارة

This is used when pointing is the best way to talk about something.

However, this is also used for other reasons:

1) To show the grandeur of something.

﴿ذَلِكَ الْكِتَابُ﴾[البقرة:٢]

This Book

2) To show the insignificance of something.

﴿أَهَذَا الَّذِي يَذْكُرُ آلِهَتَكُمْ﴾[الأنبياء:٣٦]

Is this the one who talks of your gods?

الموصول

This is used when the name of the person or thing being discussed is not known, nor can it be pointed to. For example, if you don't know a person's name and he is not around to point at, you would say something like the following to describe him, "I saw that man in the shop who we met at the masjid."

However, الموصول can be used even if the name is known. Some of the reasons for this are:

1) To show the reason for the ruling.

﴾إِنَّ الَّذِينَ يَسْتَكْبِرُونَ عَنْ عِبَادَتِي سَيَدْخُلُونَ جَهَنَّمَ دَاخِرِينَ﴿[الغافر:٦٠]

Definitely those who show arrogance against worshipping Me *shall enter Hell in disgrace.*

In this verse, the word كفار or something similar could have been used. Instead a موصول-صلة is used to show the reason of their being destined for the hell fire.

2) To point out an error.

﴾إِنَّ الَّذِينَ تَدْعُونَ مِنْ دُونِ اللَّهِ عِبَادٌ أَمْثَالُكُمْ﴿[الأعراف:١٩٤]

Surely, those whom you invoke beside Allah *are slaves (of Allah) like you.*

Instead of saying the false gods are subservient to Allah; the موصول-صلة is used to show that worshipping them is incorrect as they are mere mortals.

For example, "That man is not trustworthy" could be replaced by, "That person who you are planning on going into business with is not trustworthy". In this case the speaker is trying to point out that dealing with this person is not wise.

3) To show grandeur.

﴾فَغَشِيَهُمْ مِنَ الْيَمِّ مَا غَشِيَهُمْ﴿[طه:٧٨]

So, they were encircled by that [huge wave] *from the sea* which overwhelmed them.

4) To show insignificance.

﴾فَاقْضِ مَا أَنْتَ قَاضٍ﴿[طه:٧٢]

So, decide whatever *you have to decide*

5) To emphasise a point.

﴾وَرَاوَدَتْهُ الَّتِي هُوَ فِي بَيْتِهَا عَنْ نَفْسِهِ﴿[يوسف:٢٣]

31

And she, in whose house he was, seduced him towards herself.

In this verse Allah ﷻ is mentioning how Yusuf ﷺ kept himself away from sin and avoided the temptation to do evil. By mentioning the موصول-صلة instead of her name creates more emphasis i.e. Yusuf ﷺ abstained from committing evil with the lady in whose house he used to stay, and despite having such a close connection with her he still saved himself.

المضاف

This is used to express ownership or attribution.

رَسُوْلُ اللهِ

the prophet of Allah

However, sometimes it is used for other purposes like showing grandeur.

﴿وَاذْكُرْ عَبْدَنَا دَاوُوْدَ﴾[ص:١٧]

And remember Our servant Dawud.

By attributing the word servant to Allah it gives importance and shows high esteem.

المعرف باللام

A noun is made معرفة by adding an ال to the beginning of that word. However, the ال that precedes nouns are of varying types and carry different meaning:

1) ال: الْعَهْدِيَّة: the word عَهْد literally means to be well acquainted with. If a word has been mentioned as نكرة, then repeated, it will come as معرفة with ال العهدية.

﴿أَرْسَلْنَا إِلَى فِرْعَوْنَ رَسُولًا فَعَصَى فِرْعَوْنُ الرَّسُولَ﴾[المزمل:١٥-١٦]

We sent a messenger to Fir'awn, Then, Fir'awn disobeyed the messenger

Sometimes ال العهدية can come on a word even though the word has not been mentioned before. This is because the addressee knows who/what is being referred to.

﴿فَمَنْ حَجَّ الْبَيْتَ أَوِ اعْتَمَرَ﴾[البقرة:١٥٨]

So whoever comes to the House for Hajj or performs 'Umrah

Prior to this verse, the word بيت is not mentioned. However, everyone knows that the Ka'bah is being referred to.

2) Sometimes the ال العهدية can refer to any individual of that group. This word will be معرفة grammatically, but نكرة in meaning.

﴿أَخَافُ أَنْ يَأْكُلَهُ الذِّئْبُ﴾[يوسف:١٣]

I fear that some wolf may eat him up.

In this verse, the word الذئب has an ال on it. This ال is not referring to a specific wolf. This is why it is translated as some wolf.

33

3) الجِنْسِيَّة ال: This is used when the general meaning or concept of the word is meant, not a particular individual.

﴿وَجَعَلْنَا مِنَ الْمَاءِ كُلَّ شَيْءٍ حَيٍّ﴾ [الأنبياء: ٣٠]

We created from water every living thing.

In this verse, water is being referred to in the general sense, not any individual type of water.

4) الإسْتِغْرَاقِيَّة ال: This is used when everyone or everything is meant.

﴿إِنَّ الْإِنْسَانَ لَفِي خُسْرٍ إِلَّا الَّذِينَ آمَنُوا وَعَمِلُوا الصَّالِحَاتِ﴾ [العصر: ٢-٣]

Man is in a state of loss indeed, except those
who believed and did righteous deeds

In this verse, the word الإنسان refers to all mankind, and not one particular person.

It is worth mentioning that استغراق doesn't have to include every single individual of a particular group, it can also be limited to the topic of discussion.

﴿وَجَاءَ السَّحَرَةُ فِرْعَوْنَ﴾ [العراف: ١١٣]

The sorcerers came to Pharaoh.

The ال on the word السحرة is for استغراق, but it doesn't mean every single magician in the world, rather the magicians of Fir'awn's kingdom. This is called اِسْتِغْرَاق عُرْفِيٌّ.

نكرة

A noun is brought as نكرة when the speaker or addressee is unaware of the particular person or thing being discussed.

34

However, a word may be brought as نكرة for other reasons.

1) When there is no real benefit in mentioning it as معرفة.

﴿وَجَاءَ رَجُلٌ مِنْ أَقْصَى الْمَدِينَةِ يَسْعَى﴾[القصص:٢٠]

And there came a man running from the farthest part of the city

In this verse, the main purpose is to show that one person came to them and warned them regarding mistreating the messengers. Hence, there was no need to mention the رجل as معرفة.

2) When the speaker wishes to conceal the identity of someone.

﴿هَلْ أَدُلُّكُمْ عَلَى أَهْلِ بَيْتٍ يَكْفُلُونَهُ لَكُمْ﴾[القصص:١٢]

Shall I point out to you a family who will nurse him for you?

This sister of Musa عليه السلام did not wish to reveal the identity of her mother as that would have jeopardised Musa's عليه السلام safety; hence she kept it as نكرة.

3) The speaker may wish to keep something unspecific so the addressees may choose as they wish.

﴿اطْرَحُوهُ أَرْضًا﴾[يوسف:٩]

Throw him at some place on earth.

4) To show variety, i.e. when a plural نكرة word is brought in a sentence and the context hints towards it, the نكرة can show the meaning of كثير without actually having to add the صفة of كثير.

﴿وَلَقَدْ كُذِّبَتْ رُسُلٌ مِنْ قَبْلِكَ﴾ [الأعام:٣٤]

Indeed, many messengers have been rejected before you,

In this verse and the verses before, Allah ﷻ is consoling the Prophet ﷺ. There would be greater solace if many Prophets ﷺ had been through the same ordeal as the Prophet ﷺ. Therefore, the word *many* has been added into the translation.

5) Likewise, the نكرة may give the meaning of عظيم (great) or حقير (insignificant) in certain contexts.

﴿فَإِنْ لَمْ تَفْعَلُوا فَأْذَنُوا بِحَرْبٍ مِنَ اللَّهِ وَرَسُولِهِ﴾ [البقرة:٢٧٩]

But if you do not [give it up], then listen to the declaration of war from Allah and His Messenger.

In this verse, a warning is being issued. The context shows that war here is in the meaning of حرب عظيمة.

﴿إِنَّمَا هَذِهِ الْحَيَاةُ الدُّنْيَا مَتَاعٌ﴾ [الغافر:٣٩]

This life of the world is only a [momentary] benefit.

In this verse, the world is being showed as paltry. Hence متاع here in its نكرة form means متاع حقير.

Discussion 5
Creating Restriction

In any sentence, فعلية or إسمية, the نسبة, i.e. the link between the مسند and مسند إليه, can be restricted. This is called قَصْر. For example in a normal sentence, we will say, "Zayd is standing." However, if you want to create قصر you would say, "Only Zayd is standing."

Ways of Creating قصر

There are different ways of restricting:

1) A negative particle with the particle إلَّا.

﴿وَمَا مُحَمَّدٌ إِلَّا رَسُولٌ﴾ [آل عمران:١٤٤]

Muhammad ﷺ is but a messenger.

2) The particle إنَّمَا.

﴿إِنَّمَا نَحْنُ مُصْلِحُونَ﴾ [البقرة::١١]

We are but reformers

3) The حروف العطف of بل and لكن.

﴿قُلُوبُنَا غُلْفٌ بَلْ طَبَعَ اللّٰهُ عَلَيْهَا بِكُفْرِهِمْ﴾ [النساء:١٥٥]

"Our hearts are sealed" - rather, Allah has set a seal over them for their disbelief.

﴿وَمَا قَتَلُوهُ وَمَا صَلَبُوهُ وَلَكِنْ شُبِّهَ لَهُمْ﴾ [النساء:١٥٧]

In fact they did neither kill him, nor crucify him, but they were deluded by resemblance.

4) To make تقديم.

﴿إِيَّاكَ نَعْبُدُ وَإِيَّاكَ نَسْتَعِينُ﴾ [الفاتحة:٥]

You alone do we worship, and from You alone do we seek help.

37

Types of Qasr

The قصر can be carried out in two ways:

1) Restricting a quality to one person or being:

﴿لَا إِلَهَ إِلَّا اللَّهُ﴾ [محمد:١٩]

There is no god but Allah

In this verse the quality of being a god is restricted to a single being, Allah ﷻ.

This is called قَصْرُ الصِّفَةِ على الْمَوْصُوْفِ.

2) Restricting a person or thing to one quality:

﴿وَمَا مُحَمَّدٌ إِلَّا رَسُولٌ﴾ [آل عمران:١٤٤]

Muhammad is but a messenger

In this verse, a person, Muhammad ﷺ, is restricted to one quality.

This is called قَصْرُ الْمَوْصُوْفِ على الصِّفَةِ.

Types of Qasr: Another Angle

The قصر created by these particles can be divided into two types:

قَصْرٌ حَقِيْقِيٌّ: This is where the restriction is absolute and not relative.

﴿لَا إِلَهَ إِلَّا اللَّهُ﴾ [محمد:١٩]

There is no god but Allah ﷻ.

In this verse the restriction of god to a single being is absolute i.e. there is no god but Allah ﷻ.

قَصْرٌ إِضَافِيٌّ: This is where the restriction is relative and not absolute.

﴿وَمَا مُحَمَّدٌ إِلَّا رَسُولٌ﴾ [آل عمران:١٤٤]

Muhammad ﷺ is but a messenger.

In this example, the restriction of Muhammad to being a prophet is not absolute, because he possesses other qualities like being a father, a husband, a leader, a teacher etc. This verse restricts him to being a prophet relative to him being an eternal being. The reason for this revelation was when rumours of the his death spread and some people lost hope, Allah ﷻ educated them that he is only a prophet, not an eternal being.

If the قصر is for موصوف على الصفة it will always be إضافي because no being can have only one quality.

Discussion 6
A Few Details About حرف العطف

In this section we are going to discuss a few rules about the حرف العطف of و. The other حروف العطف will not be discussed here.

As you have studied in Nahw, this particle is used to join two or more words, phrases or sentences together. Here we are only going to discuss joining sentences together.

Usually two or more sentences are joined together with the particle و.

In this case, we would say there is وَصْل between the two sentences.

﴿ إِيَّاكَ نَعْبُدُ وَإِيَّاكَ نَسْتَعِينُ ﴾ [الفاتحة:٥-٦]

*You alone do we worship, and from You alone
do we seek help.*

However, sometimes two sentences may come together without the particle و, or any other حرف العطف for that matter. In this case, we would say there is فَصْل between the two sentences.

There are two main reasons for فصل.

1) The first is when the second sentence is very closely linked to the first. This happens when:

    a. the second sentence is a بَدل to the first

﴿ وَاتَّقُوا الَّذِي أَمَدَّكُم بِمَا تَعْلَمُونَ أَمَدَّكُم بِأَنْعَامٍ وَبَنِينَ وَجَنَّاتٍ وَعُيُونٍ ﴾ [الشعراء:١٣١-١٣٤]

*And fear the One who has supported you with
what you know. He has supported you with
cattle and sons, and with gardens and springs.*

40

In this verse the words أَمَدَّكُم بِأَنْعَامٍ وَبَنِينَ وَجَنَّاتٍ وَعُيُونٍ is a بدل
for the sentence before it; أَمَدَّكُم بِمَا تَعْلَمُونَ.

b. the second sentence is a بيان for the first i.e. it
explains or clarifies the first.

﴿فَوَسْوَسَ إِلَيْهِ الشَّيْطَانُ قَالَ يَا آدَمُ هَلْ أَدُلُّكَ عَلَى شَجَرَةِ الْخُلْدِ﴾[طه:١٢٠]

Then the Satan instigated him. *He said, "Adam,
shall I guide you to the tree of eternity."*

c. the second sentence is a توكيد for the first

﴿مَا هَذَا بَشَرًا إِنْ هَذَا إِلَّا مَلَكٌ كَرِيمٌ﴾ [يوسف:١٣١]

He is no human being. *He is but a noble angel.*

In such instances we would say there is كَمَالُ الِاتِّصَال
between the two sentences.

2) The second place where there is no need for a و of عطف
is when the second sentence is like an answer to a
question which may arise from the first.

﴿وَمَا أُبَرِّئُ نَفْسِي إِنَّ النَّفْسَ لَأَمَّارَةٌ بِالسُّوءِ﴾ [يوسف:٥٣]

And I do not absolve my inner self of blame.
Surely, man's inner self often incites to evil.

After the first sentence a question could be posed:
"Why do you not absolve you inner self of blame?"
The sentence after it answers that.

In such instances we would say there is شِبْهُ كَمَالِ الِاتِّصَال
between the two sentences.

Discussion 7
Length of Speech

A speaker may choose one of three ways to express what he wishes to say:

1. مُسَاوَاة: a moderate way which is neither too brief nor too long.

2. إِيْجَاز: a concise manner.

3. إِطْنَابٌ: a lengthy manner.

مُسَاوَاةٌ

Most of the verses of the Quran are مساواة.

﴿وَمَنْ يُطِعِ اللَّهَ وَرَسُولَهُ يُدْخِلْهُ جَنَّاتٍ تَجْرِي مِنْ تَحْتِهَا الْأَنْهَارُ خَالِدِينَ فِيهَا وَذَلِكَ الْفَوْزُ الْعَظِيمُ﴾ [النساء:١٣]

Whoever obeys Allah and His Messenger, He will admit him to gardens beneath which rivers flow, where he will live forever. That is a great success.

إِيْجَازٌ

There are two types of إِيْجَاز. One is called إِيْجَاز قَصْر. This is where the choice of words is such that it encompasses a very vast meaning. An example of this is the description of Heaven:

﴿وَلَكُمْ فِيهَا مَا تَشْتَهِي أَنْفُسُكُمْ﴾ [فصلت:٣١]

And for you in Heaven is whatever your souls desire.

42

Even though the words of this verse are a few, its meaning is very extensive.

The second type of إيجاز is called إِيجَازُ حَذْفٍ. This is to remove sentences or parts of sentences.

The مَحْذُوف, the removed part, can be one of the following:

1) مبتدأ

﴿وَمَا أَدْرَاكَ مَا هِيَهْ، ... نَارٌ حَامِيَةٌ ﴾[القارعة:١٠]

And what may let you know what that is? [It is]
A blazing Fire!

2) خبر

﴿أُكُلُهَا دَائِمٌ وَظِلُّهَا ...﴾[الرعد:٣٥]

Its food is everlasting and its shade [is also
everlasting].

3) فاعل

﴿إِذَا بَلَغَتِ ... التَّرَاقِيَ﴾[القيامة:٢٦]

When [the soul] reaches to the collar bone.

4) مفعول

﴿فَذُوقُوا ... بِمَا نَسِيتُمْ لِقَاءَ يَوْمِكُمْ هَذَا﴾[السجدة:١٤]

Then taste you [the torment of the Fire]
because of your forgetting the Meeting of this
Day of yours.

5) حرف

﴿... تَفْتَأُ تَذْكُرُ يُوسُفَ﴾[يوسف:٣٥]

By God, you will not stop remembering Yusuf.

The فعل ناقص of تفتأ is always brought in the negative i.e. مَا فَتِئَ or لَا يَفْتَئُ. Here the particle لا has been removed.

6) مضاف

﴿وَاسْأَلِ ... الْقَرْيَةَ﴾ [يوسف:٨٣]

Ask [the people of] the town.

7) جار-مجرور

﴿وَلَذِكْرُ اللَّهِ أَكْبَرُ ...﴾[العنكبوت:٤٥]

Indeed remembrance of Allah is greater [than all things].

8) موصوف

﴿وَعِنْدَهُمْ ... قَاصِرَاتُ الطَّرْفِ﴾[الصافات:٤٨]

And by their side there will be (wives) lowering their gazes.

9) صفة

﴿الَّذِي أَطْعَمَهُمْ مِنْ جُوعٍ ...﴾[القريش:٤]

Who gave them food against [severe] hunger.
This links back to the نكرة giving the meaning of عظيم or حقير.

10) جواب الشرط

﴿قُلْ أَرَأَيْتُمْ إِنْ كَانَ مِنْ عِنْدِ اللَّهِ ثُمَّ كَفَرْتُمْ بِهِ...﴾ [فصلت:٥٢]

"Tell me, if it [the Qur'an] is from Allah, and still you reject it...

11) Sentence or sentences

﴿إِنِّي آمَنْتُ بِرَبِّكُمْ فَاسْمَعُونِ قِيلَ ادْخُلِ الْجَنَّةَ﴾ [يس:٢٥]

Undoubtedly I have believed in your Lord; so listen to me." [Thereafter when his people killed him] it was said to him, "Enter the Paradise."

44

إطْنَاب, lengthening a sentence can occur in one of the following ways:

1) ذِكْرُ الخَاصِّ بَعْدَ الْعَامِ: to mention something specifically after something general which already includes it.

﴿حَافِظُوا عَلَى الصَّلَوَاتِ وَالصَّلَاةِ الْوُسْطَى﴾ [البقرة:٢٣٨]

Take due care of all the prayers, and the middle prayer.

The word الصلوات includes all prayers, but the الصَّلَاةِ الْوُسْطَى is mentioned specifically to emphasise it.

2) ذِكْرُ الْعَامِ بَعْدَ الخَاصِّ: to mention something generally even though it has been mentioned specifically before.

﴿رَبِّ اغْفِرْ لِي وَلِوَالِدَيَّ وَلِمَنْ دَخَلَ بَيْتِيَ مُؤْمِنًا وَلِلْمُؤْمِنِينَ وَالْمُؤْمِنَاتِ﴾ [نوح:٢٨]

My Lord, grant pardon to me, and to my parents, and to everyone who enters my home as a believer, and to all the believing men and believing women.

3) تَكْرَار: to repeat something

﴿فَبِأَيِّ آلَاءِ رَبِّكُمَا تُكَذِّبَانِ﴾ [الرحمن:١٣]

So, which of the bounties of your Lord will you deny?

This is mentioned 31 times in the chapter.

4) تَذْيِيل: This means to bring a sentence after another sentence to emphasise it. In this case both will have the same message.

﴿جَاءَ الْحَقُّ وَزَهَقَ الْبَاطِلُ إِنَّ الْبَاطِلَ كَانَ زَهُوقًا﴾ [الإسراء:٨٠]

45

Truth has come and falsehood has vanished.
Falsehood is surely bound to vanish.

5) إِحْتِرَاسٌ: This means to add something which prevents the wrong meaning being taken.

﴿وَاضْمُمْ يَدَكَ إِلَى جَنَاحِكَ تَخْرُجْ بَيْضَاءَ مِنْ غَيْرِ سُوءٍ﴾[طه:٢٢]

Press your hand under your arm, and it will
come out [brightly] white without any disease.

This prevents someone interpreting the whiteness of his hand as an illness.

6) تَتْمِيمٌ: This means to add something which increases the meaning.

﴿وَيُطْعِمُونَ الطَّعَامَ عَلَى حُبِّهِ مِسْكِينًا وَيَتِيمًا وَأَسِيرًا﴾[الإنسان:٨]

And they give food, out of their love for Him
(Allah), to the needy, and the orphan, and the
captive.

7) إِعْتَرَاض: This means to bring a sentence within another sentence.

﴿وَيَجْعَلُونَ لِلَّهِ الْبَنَاتِ سُبْحَانَهُ وَلَهُمْ مَا يَشْتَهُونَ﴾[النحل:٥٧]

They ascribe daughters to Allah - Pure is He -
and for themselves is what they desire!

46

Discussion 8
A Few Miscellaneous Rules

In this section we are going to discuss a few miscellaneous rules.

1) اَلْإِضْمَارُ مَقَامَ الْإِظْهَارِ: The general rule is that a pronoun of غائب is only used after the noun has been mentioned previously. However, a ضمير of غائب can be brought even without the noun being mentioned before. This is done to show that the noun is fixed in the mind and does need to be mentioned to be understood.

﴿الم ۝ تَنْزِيلُ الْكِتَابِ لَا رَيْبَ فِيهِ مِنْ رَبِّ الْعَالَمِينَ ۝ أَمْ يَقُولُونَ افْتَرَاهُ﴾
[السجدة: ١-٣]

(This) revelation of the Book - in which there is no doubt - is from the Lord of the worlds. Is it that they (the disbelievers) *say, "He (Muhammad ﷺ) has fabricated it."*

2) اَلْإِظْهَارُ مَقَامَ الْإِضْمَارِ: When something has been mentioned once as a noun, it is usually mentioned again as a pronoun. However, sometimes the noun is repeated. There are many reasons for this. One is to show the grandeur of something.

﴿الْقَارِعَةُ مَا الْقَارِعَةُ وَمَا أَدْرَاكَ مَا الْقَارِعَةُ﴾[القارعة: ١-٣]

The Striking Event! What is the Striking Event? And what may let you know what the Striking Event is?

47

After the word القارعة has been mentioned once, it could have been replaced with the pronoun هي. But to show how great القارعة is, the noun is repeated again twice.

3) إلْتِفَات: This is when the speaker changes his speech from 1st person to 2nd person etc.

﴿وَمَا لِيَ لَا أَعْبُدُ الَّذِي فَطَرَنِي وَإِلَيْهِ تُرْجَعُونَ ﴾[يس:٢٢]

What excuse do I have if I do not worship the One who has created me *and* to whom you will be returned?

4) تَجَاهُلُ الْعَارِفِ: This means that the speaker speaks as though he is unaware of something even though he is aware.

﴿وَإِنَّا أَوْ إِيَّاكُمْ لَعَلَى هُدًى أَوْ فِي ضَلَالٍ مُبِينٍ﴾[سبأ:٢٤]

And We or you are either *on the right path or in open error."*

Secition 2

عِلْمُ الْبَيَانِ

In this section we are going to discuss similes and metaphors.

التَّشْبِيهُ

A simile is a figure of speech where two things are compared.

This lesson is as easy as ABC.

In Arabic, a simile is called تَشْبِيهٌ.

A تشبيه is made up of four parts:

1) مُشَبَّةٌ: This is the thing being compared.

2) مُشَبَّةٌ بِهِ: This is the thing that is being compared to.

3) أَدَاةُ التَّشْبِيهِ: This is the word used to draw comparison.

4) وَجْهُ الشَّبْهِ: This is the common factor between the مشبه and مشبه به.

The Quran is like light in the way it guides.

In this example, *the Quran* is the مشبه, the word *light* is مشبه به, the word *like* is the أداة التشبيه and *the way it guides* is وجه الشبه.

Here is an examples of تشبيه from the Quran.

﴿ يَخْرُجُونَ مِنَ الْأَجْدَاثِ كَأَنَّهُمْ جَرَادٌ مُنْتَشِرٌ ﴾ [القمر: ٧]

They will come out of the graves like locusts spread all over.

Even though there are four parts to a تشبيه, it is very seldom that all four will be mentioned. The core of these four are مشبه and مشبه به, and every تشبيه must have these. The second two, أداة التشبيه and وجه الشبه are secondary and either one of them, and in some cases both of them, can be removed from the sentence even though they will still exist in the background.

If the وجه الشبه is not mentioned the تشبيه will be called تَشْبِيهٌ مُجْمَلٌ.

﴿كَأَنَّهُمْ حُمُرٌ مُسْتَنْفِرَةٌ فَرَّتْ مِنْ قَسْوَرَةٍ﴾ [المُدَّثِّرٌ: ٥٠]

As if they were wild donkeys, Fleeing from a lion.

If the أداة التشبيه is not mentioned the تشبيه is called تَشْبِيهٌ مُؤَكَّدٌ.

«الْمُؤْمِنُ مِرْآةُ الْمُؤْمِنِ، وَالْمُؤْمِنُ أَخُو الْمُؤْمِنِ، يَكُفُّ عَلَيْهِ ضَيْعَتَهُ، وَيَحُوطُهُ مِنْ وَرَائِهِ» [أبو داؤود]

A believer is the mirror of a believer … He protects him against loss and defends him behind his back.

In this example, a believer is likened to a mirror, but the أداة التشبيه has been removed. It was originally "A believer is like the mirror of his brother", but to make the simile more emphatic the أداة التشبيه is removed.

If both the وجه الشبه and أداة التشبيه are not mentioned, the تشبيه will be called تَشْبِيهٌ بَلِيغٌ.

«وَالصَّلَاةُ نُورٌ، وَالصَّدَقَةُ بُرْهَانٌ وَالصَّبْرُ ضِيَاءٌ» [مسلم]

And the salah (prayer) is a light, and charity is a proof, and patience is illumination,

Another very delicate تشبيه is تَشْبِيهٌ مَقْلُوبٌ. This is where the مشبه and مشبه به are swapped around to give the impression that the original مشبه possesses the quality more than the original مشبه به.

﴿إِنَّمَا الْبَيْعُ مِثْلُ الرِّبَا﴾ [البقرة: ٢٧٥]

Trade is just like usury

In this verse a saying of the disbelievers is quoted in which they try to justify their practice of usury. Their claim was that usury is just like a normal transaction. The verse should have read like this "Usury is just like trade". Instead they switched it around giving the impression that trade should be compared to the usury and not the other way around.

المجاز

A metaphor, مَجَاز, is a figure of speech similar to a simile, تشبيه. However, it goes one step further than تشبيه by removing the مشبه all together. Look at the example below.

The wall is not playing today.

This is a مجاز which originates from a تشبيه. The تشبيه would have been "This player is like a wall in defence." In the مجاز the مشبه, this player, is removed all together and the مشبه به is used in its place.

This type of مجاز is called إِسْتِعَارَةٌ.

الاستعارة

الاستعارة means to merge a تشبيه to the extent that the مشبه becomes diluted into the مشبه به.

The following verse of the Quran is an example of إستعارة.

﴿كِتَابٌ أَنْزَلْنَاهُ إِلَيْكَ لِتُخْرِجَ النَّاسَ مِنَ الظُّلُمَاتِ إِلَى النُّورِ﴾ [إبراهيم: ١]

This is a book We have sent down to you, so that you may deliver the people, with the will of their Lord, out of all sorts of darkness *into the* light.

This إستعارة originates from two تشبيه which could be assumed to be something like:

الضَّلَالَةُ مِثْلُ الظُّلُمَاتِ   الهِدَايَةُ مِثْلُ النُّورِ

From these تشبيه the مشبه was removed and only the مشبه به remained.

Types of إِسْتِعَارَة

إستعارة can be divided into two types:

1) اَلْمُصَرَّحَةُ: This is where the مشبه به of the original تشبيه is mentioned.

﴿كِتَابٌ أَنْزَلْنَاهُ إِلَيْكَ لِتُخْرِجَ النَّاسَ مِنَ الظُّلُمَاتِ إِلَى النُّورِ﴾ [إبراهيم: ١]

2) اَلْمَكْنِيَّةُ: This is where the إِسْتِعَارَة has become so strong that now even the مشبه به is not mentioned, rather something relevant to the مشبه به is mentioned.

﴿وَإِذَا الْكَوَاكِبُ انْتَثَرَتْ﴾ [الإنفطار: ٢]

And when the stars will disperse.

In this verse the verb انتثر is used. This verb is originally used to express the scattering of rosary beads when its thread is cut. An إستعارة is used here without even mentioning the مشبه به; instead something related to it is mentioned. The original تشبيه would be assumed to be something like this: the planets and stars in their orbit are like rosary beads on a thread.

53

If an إستعارة carries on to mention more things related to the مشبه به, this is called ترشيح.

Once Khabbab Ibn al-Aratt ﷺ sat reflecting at how Allah ﷻ had given him so many gifts of the world whilst some of his friends passed away without seeing any of the gifts he enjoyed. One of the sentences he used was:

مِنَّا مَنْ أَيْنَعَتْ لَهُ ثَمَرَتُهُ فَهُوَ يَهْدِبُهَا

Some of us have had their fruits ripened [in this world] and they are harvesting them.

The origin of this إستعارة is a تشبيه i.e. striving is like planting seeds. Then the مشبه, striving, was removed and the مشبه به remained. Then the مشبه به was removed and aspects related to it were mentioned, like fruits and ripening. He then goes on to add a ترشيح by saying "they are harvesting them."

Here is a recap of تشبيه and إستعارة in order of how eloquent they are:

تشبيه	
تشبيه مؤكد	تشبيه مجمل
تشبيه بليغ	
إستعارة مصرحة	
إستعارة مكنية	
إستعارة مرشحة	

Another type of إستعارة is one in which a complete sentence is used to draw similitude between two things. For example, in the saying, "You are opening a can of worms," there isn't a single word used as إستعارة, rather the entire phrase is used to draw similitude with someone doing something which could have severe repercussions.

﴿مَا مِنْ دَابَّةٍ إِلَّا هُوَ آخِذٌ بِنَاصِيَتِهَا﴾ [هود:٥٦]

There is no creature but He holds it by the forelock.

This entire verse means that Allah ﷻ has total control over every creation.

المجاز العقلي

This is when a مسند is not attributed to its real مسند إليه.

﴿ إِنَّ فِرْعَوْنَ عَلَا فِي الْأَرْضِ وَجَعَلَ أَهْلَهَا شِيَعًا يَسْتَضْعِفُ طَائِفَةً مِنْهُمْ يُذَبِّحُ أَبْنَاءَهُمْ وَيَسْتَحْيِي نِسَاءَهُمْ﴾ [القصص:٤]

Indeed, Fir'awn had become high-handed in the land, and had divided its people into different groups; he used to persecute a group of them, slaughtering their sons and keeping their women alive.

Fir'awn himself didn't carry out the slaughtering, but because he instructed his men to do so the act is attributed to him.

55

This is a مجاز in which a word is replaced by another, similar to إستعارة. However, in إستعارة, the reason for using the alternative word was تشبيه; whilst in المجاز المرسل the reason is one of the following:

1) اَلسَّبَبِيَّة: This is where the cause of something is mentioned in its place.

«ٱلْمُسْلِمُ مَنْ سَلِمَ الْمُسْلِمُونَ مِنْ لِسَانِهِ وَيَدِهِ»

A Muslim is the one from whose tongue and hands the Muslims are safe.

Here hands and tongue are used in place of actions and words; tongue and hands being the cause.

2) اَلْمُسَبَّبِيَّة: This is where the result of something is mentioned in its place:

﴿وَيُنَزِّلُ لَكُم مِنَ السَّمَاءِ رِزْقًا﴾[غافر:١٣]

And He sends down provision for you from the sky.

Here the word provisions refer to rain; provision being the result of rain.

3) الكُلِّيَّة: This is where all of something is mentioned instead of a part:

﴿ يَجْعَلُونَ أَصَابِعَهُمْ فِي آذَانِهِمْ ﴾ [البقرة:١٩]

They thrust their fingers in their ears.

Here the word fingers is mentioned, but it actually refers to finger tips.

4) الْجُزْئِيَّة: This is where a part of something is mentioned instead of the entire thing.

﴿ تَحْرِيرُ رَقَبَةٍ ﴾ [المائدة:٨٩]

Freeing of a neck.

Here neck refers to the entire body i.e. freeing a slave.

5) إِعْتِبَارُ مَا كَانَ: This is where something is mentioned by what it was instead of what it is.

﴿وَآتُوا الْيَتَامَى أَمْوَالَهُمْ﴾ [النساء:٢]

Give the orphans their property.

An orphan is a child whose parents have passed away. In this verse, the guardians are instructed to give the orphans their property after they have matured. Once they have matured, they are not really orphans. So here orphan really means those who were orphans.

6) إِعْتِبَارُ مَا يَكُونُ: This is where something is mentioned by what it will be instead of what it is.

﴿إِنِّي أَرَانِي أَعْصِرُ خَمْرًا﴾ [يوسف:٣٦]

I have seen myself [in dream] pressing wine.

Wine is a finished product. Pressing actually takes place on the grapes from which the wine is made. Here, the grapes are called wine because they will become wine.

This is when something is used in a way that the original meaning is not intended, even if it could be taken.

I don't have blood on my hands.

The purpose of this sentence is to state that the speaker is innocent and has not committed anything wrong. Even though the literal meaning is correct it is not intended.

﴿قَالَتْ رَبِّ أَنَّىٰ يَكُونُ لِي وَلَدٌ وَلَمْ يَمْسَسْنِي بَشَرٌ﴾ [آل عمران:٤٧]

Maryam said, "O my Lord, how shall I have a son while no human has ever touched me?"

In this statement she is not referring to a normal touch, rather she means to say I have never cohabited.

Another example of this is the following statement of the Prophet ﷺ:

»أَسْرَعُكُنَّ لَحَاقًا بِي أَطْوَلُكُنَّ يَدًا« [مسلم]

The one who has the longest hands amongst you [the wives of the Prophet ﷺ] will meet me most immediately.

The Prophet ﷺ did not intend the literal meaning of having long hands; rather he meant the one who is most generous.

Section 3

عِلْمُ الْبَدِيْعُ

This science refers to those things which create a beauty within the sentence without which the meaning of the sentence wouldn't change. These embellishments, مُحَسَّنَاتٌ, can be divided into two categories:

1) مُحَسَّنَاتٌ لَفْظِيَّةٌ: These relate to those embellishments which create beauty within the words of the sentence.

2) مُحَسَّنَاتٌ مَعْنَوِيَّةٌ: These relate to those embellishments which create beauty within the meaning of the sentence.

مُحَسَّنَاتٌ لَفْظِيَّةٌ

Here are some of the محسنات لفظية:

1) بَرَاعَةُ الْاِسْتِهْلَالِ: This is to start a text, a poem or chapter with something spectacular:

﴿سُبْحَانَ الَّذِي أَسْرَى بِعَبْدِهِ لَيْلًا مِنَ الْمَسْجِدِ الْحَرَامِ إِلَى الْمَسْجِدِ الْأَقْصَى الَّذِي بَارَكْنَا حَوْلَهُ﴾ [الإسراء:١]

Glorious is He Who made his servant travel by night from Al-Masjid-ul-Haram to Al-Masjid-ul-Aqsa whose environs We have blessed.

2) حُسْنُ الْخِتَامِ: To end of a text with something nice.

﴿وَآخِرُ دَعْوَاهُمْ أَنِ الْحَمْدُ لِلَّهِ رَبِّ الْعَالَمِينَ﴾ [يونس:١٠]

And the end of their call will be, "Praise be to Allah, the Lord of all the worlds."

3) رَدُّ الصَّدْرِ عَلَى الْعَجْزِ: This means to end the speech with something similar to which it started.

﴿وَتَخْشَى النَّاسَ وَاللَّهُ أَحَقُّ أَنْ تَخْشَاهُ﴾ [الاحزاب:٣٧]

You were fearing people, while Allah is more entitled to be feared by you.

This can occur at the start and end of a chapter as well. For example, the chapter of The Pen starts by negating the claims that the Prophet ﷺ is insane and it ends on the same note.

﴿ن وَالْقَلَمِ وَمَا يَسْطُرُونَ مَا أَنتَ بِنِعْمَةِ رَبِّكَ بِمَجْنُونٍ﴾ [القلم: ٢-١]

By the pen and what they write, with the grace of your Lord, you are not insane.

﴿ وَيَقُولُونَ إِنَّهُ لَمَجْنُونٌ وَمَا هُوَ إِلَّا ذِكْرٌ لِلْعَالَمِينَ﴾ [القلم: ٥٢]

And they say, "He is a madman indeed." And it is nothing else but a Reminder for all the worlds.

4) اَلسَّجَعُ: This is where each sentence ends on a similar pattern:

﴿طه ⟳ مَا أَنْزَلْنَا عَلَيْكَ الْقُرْآنَ لِتَشْقَى ⟳ إِلَّا تَذْكِرَةً لِمَنْ يَخْشَى ⟳ تَنْزِيلًا مِّمَّنْ خَلَقَ الْأَرْضَ وَالسَّمَاوَاتِ الْعُلَى ⟳ الرَّحْمَنُ عَلَى الْعَرْشِ اسْتَوَى ⟳ لَهُ مَا فِي السَّمَاوَاتِ وَمَا فِي الْأَرْضِ وَمَا بَيْنَهُمَا وَمَا تَحْتَ الثَّرَى ⟳ وَإِنْ تَجْهَرْ بِالْقَوْلِ فَإِنَّهُ يَعْلَمُ السِّرَّ وَأَخْفَى ⟳ اللَّهُ لَا إِلَهَ إِلَّا هُوَ لَهُ الْأَسْمَاءُ الْحُسْنَى ⟳﴾
[طه: ١-٨]

5) اَلْجِنَاس: This is when words with similar pronunciations but different meanings are brought together.

﴿وَيَوْمَ تَقُومُ السَّاعَةُ يُقْسِمُ الْمُجْرِمُونَ مَا لَبِثُوا غَيْرَ سَاعَةٍ﴾ [الروم: ٥٥]

And on the Day when the Hour [Qiyamah: the Day of Judgement] will take place, the sinners will swear that they did not remain [in the graves] more than one hour.

6) اَلْقَلْب: This is when a sentence can be read both forwards and backwards.

﴿كُلٌّ فِي فَلَكٍ﴾ [يس:٤٠]

Each one in an orbit.

مُحَسِّنَاتٌ مَعْنَوِيَّةٌ

1) الطِّبَاقُ: This is to bring opposite things together. The opposites can be:

Nouns:

﴿هُوَ الْأَوَّلُ وَالْآخِرُ وَالظَّاهِرُ وَالْبَاطِنُ﴾ [الحديد:٣]

He is the First and the Last, and the Manifest and the Hidden.

Verbs:

﴿وَأَنَّهُ هُوَ أَضْحَكَ وَأَبْكَى ۝ وَأَنَّهُ هُوَ أَمَاتَ وَأَحْيَا﴾ [النجم:٤٣]

And that He is the One who makes [one] laugh and makes [him] weep, and that He is the One who gives death and gives life.

Mixture:

﴿وَمَنْ يُضْلِلِ اللَّهُ فَمَا لَهُ مِنْ هَادٍ﴾ [الرعد:٣٣]

The one whom Allah deprives of guidance, there is no one to guide.

2) مُرَاعَاةُ النَّظِيرِ: This means to bring similar things together.

﴿الشَّمْسُ وَالْقَمَرُ بِحُسْبَانٍ﴾ [الرحمان:٥]

The sun and the moon are [bound] by a [fixed] calculation

3) الْمُشَاكَلَةُ: This means to express a meaning via a word which it is not usually used for. This is done because of the two words coming together in the text.

﴿فَمَنِ اعْتَدَى عَلَيْكُمْ فَاعْتَدُوا عَلَيْهِ بِمِثْلِ مَا اعْتَدَى عَلَيْكُمْ﴾ [البقرة:١٩٤]

Whoever transgresses the prohibition against
you, you transgress likewise against him.

The word transgresses literally means to break a law. This ayah states that if someone were to do wrong against another, the wronged is entitled to take is due right even if the transgressor undergoes loss. In the second sentence, the word اعتدى, transgression, is used to express the meaning of taking one's due right only because the same word has been mentioned in the previous sentence.

4) التَّوْرِيَةُ: This is to use a sentence which can have two meanings. The listener takes one meaning whilst the speaker intends another. For example, on the migration from Makkah to Madeenah, when anyone would meet Abu Bakr and ask him regarding his companion, the Prophet Muhammad ﷺ, he would say:

هَذَا الرَّجُلُ يَهْدِينِي السَّبِيلَ [البخاري]

He is a man who shows me the path.

The listener would assume he meant a guide whilst he meant the one who shows me the way to good.

5) تَأْكِيدُ الْمَدْحِ بِمَا يُشْبِهُ الذَّمَّ: This is to emphasise a praise in such a way that it seems as though it is criticism.

﴿لَا يَسْمَعُونَ فِيهَا لَغْوًا وَلَا تَأْثِيمًا إِلَّا قِيلًا سَلَامًا سَلَامًا﴾ [الواقعة ٢٥-٢٦]

They will hear neither an absurd talk in heaven,
nor something leading to sin, but [they will
hear] the words of Salam, Salam [as greetings].

In this verse when the word إِلَّا is brought, one automatically thinks that something bad is going to be mentioned.

This creates emphasis because it implies that there is nothing bad to be heard in Heaven except this one thing; and because this is also good it means everything heard in heaven will be good.

6) تَأْكِيدُ الذَّمِ بِمَا يُشْبِهُ الْمَدْحَ: This is to emphasise a criticism in such a way that it seems as though it is praise:

﴿ فَلَا صَدَّقَ وَلَا صَلَّى وَلَكِنْ كَذَّبَ وَتَوَلَّى﴾ [القيامة ٣١-٣٢]

So [the denier of the Hereafter] neither believed, nor prayed, but rejected the truth and turned away [from it].

Again, in this verse, when the word but is mentioned it appears as though something good is going to be mentioned. On the contrary, another bad quality is mentioned implying that everything about him is evil.